How to Ride Pegasus
an illustrated guide to balanced seat riding

Published by
AKA-Publishing
Columbia, MO 65203

ISBN 978-1-942168-19-5 Trade Paperback

How to Ride Pegasus
an illustrated guide to balanced seat riding

Written and illustrated by
Leslie McCullough-Payne

So, you want to ride Pegasus. Good for you!
It's nice to have a dream or two.
A dream can come true if you are willing to believe,
and turn away from doubt, fear, or need.

The following book is an illustrated guide to balanced seat riding.

By doing these exercises on your horse or pony, you will be able to ride in rhythm with the movement of your horse or pony and soon will be ready to fly.

I do recommend riding bareback because no saddle fits on Pegasus, and it is easier to feel the horse's movements.

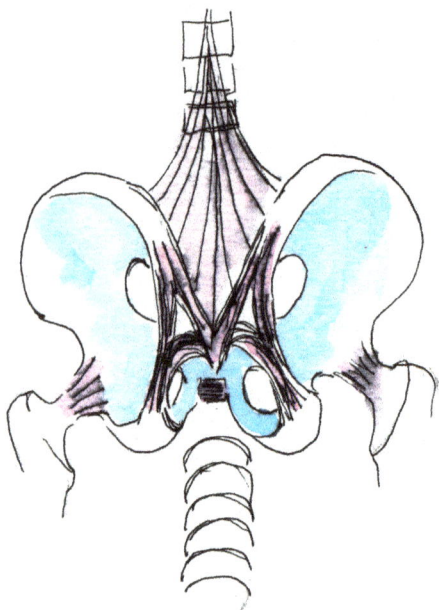

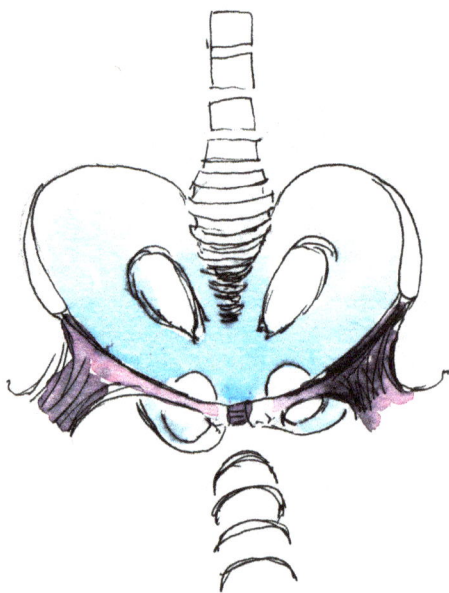

First, lets look at your bones.

Your hips are a combination of bone, tendons, and ligaments. Your spine comes down between the "wings" of the hip and ends in the tail bone, which is actually several small bones fused together.

The most comfortable place for your spine to be is directly over the horse's spine. A triangular base is formed with the bottom parts of your hip. Sit on a chair, put your hand under you bottom and rock side to side, you will feel your back pelvic bones, (seat bones). Your front seat bone has lighter contact with the horse's back. It is the bone you feel in front when you put your hand where your legs meet. Your tail bone is used to increase and decrease the pressure of the other seat bones.

All your seat bones move with the horse's movements in such a subtle way that most people do not notice.

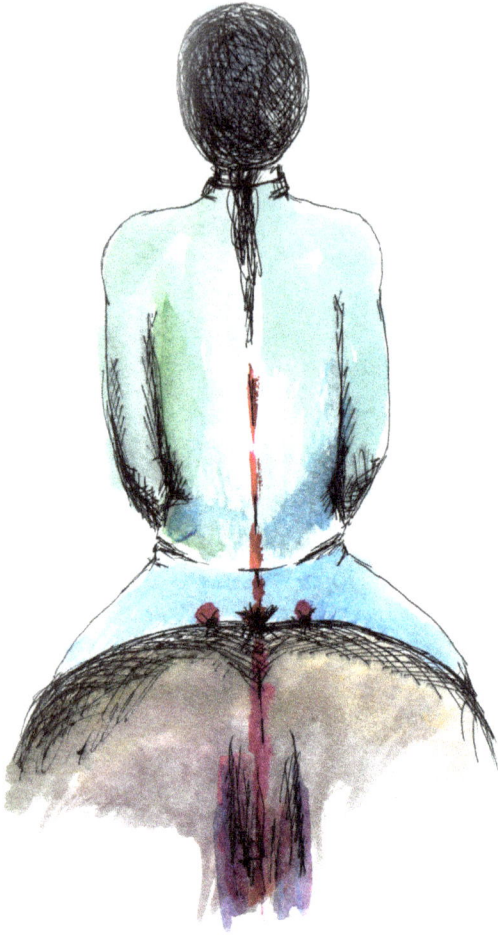

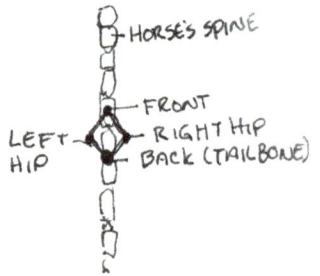

HORSE'S SPINE

FRONT

LEFT HIP — RIGHT HIP

BACK (TAILBONE)

It is most important to keep your spine in line with the horse's spine and to have a knowledge of the weight distribution between your seat bones.

The horse moves toward weight, so if you put more weight on your right seat bone, the horse will travel toward the right. Remember, and use this approach to direct your horse.

Try placing your hand on the horse's back, behind your seat. Feel the horse's hips move. Now, feel how your seat bones move with the horse's movement.

Next, don't allow your seat bones to move. Did your horse raise his head a bit? Did he stop?

Now, allow or even increase the movement of your seat bones in rhythm with the horse's movements. Did your horse's head lower? Did he increase the speed of his walk, or start to trot?

This is one way of communicating with your horse. Play with this at the walk, trot or jog, and canter or lope.

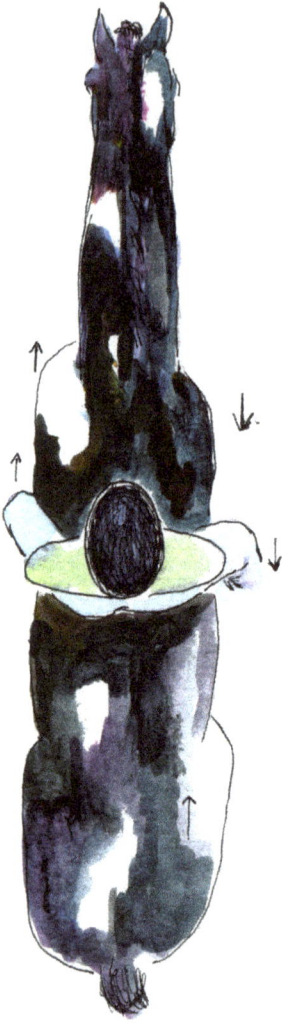

Watch your horse's shoulders move back and forth.

The horse's shoulders move in a circular motion just like you rolling or circling your shoulders.

Next, allow your legs to swing slightly forward and back with the movement of your horse's shoulders.

Now "march" with your knees, allowing the swinging motion to lift your knee up, forward, and back again. This is not a big movement, but you will notice a response in your horse, as he will go forward in a more relaxed and willing manner.

Now stop and restrict the movement of you legs and knees. What did your horse do?

Relax and move with the horse's rhythm again. Notice the difference. Do this at all three gaits.

Try the next exercise while your horse is standing still, then progress to doing it while he is walking, then jogging or trotting, and then the lope or canter.

Bending in the hip joint and keeping your back straight, bring your chest to your horse's neck and sit back up again. Make sure your legs do not swing backwards. Sometimes it helps to put your hands on your hips or lower back to make sure you are not just bending from your waist. Bending from your waist can make you roll over the horse's shoulders.

Next, bend backwards, bringing your head to the horse's back and bring yourself back up to sitting. Make sure your legs do not move forward, and only go as far as is comfortable for your back. This is not an easy exercise! With practice it gets easier and easier, and can become a fluid back and forth motion with time. It is most important to keep your legs in place, not by clinching, but by building the strength and flexibility needed for the exercise.

Have fun with this exercise and make it a game. Do not be upset if you slide off your horse sometimes. Finding the ground or sliding off is a part of riding and why we wear helmets.

Now investigate trunk twisters and side to sides.

First, make sure your are centered over the horse's back, then hold your arms out at shoulder height and slowly rotate so that your hands are above the horse's neck and hindquarters, feel the twist in your waist, slowly rotate back and then to the other direction.

If you shift the weight on your seat bones, the horse will start traveling toward the weight, so keep those bones evenly weighted or you will be walking circles.

Next, try side to side. Again, make sure you are centered, then hold your arms at shoulder height, bring your right hand toward your right knee while your left hand reaches to the sky. Repeat to the left. You must keep the weight even in your seat bones or you will find yourself sliding to the side. Horses like to play just like all of us, so if you do slide he will most likely, step out from under you and you will find the ground.

Keep playing at this exercise, expand it to touching your knees or toes on each side, and then combining it with the trunk twisters, touch the right hand to the left knee or even toe.

With practice, you will be able to do this at all three gaits.

A test for how even you keep the weight between your seat bones is riding sidesaddle. Yes, you can do this bareback.

To counter balance the weight of the leg going across the horse withers (the ridge between the shoulder blades), you must move the seat bone and shoulder of your crossing leg back a bit. Lift up through your waist and keep your spine coming straight up from the horse's spine.

Play with this and try it at different gaits, but stay safe. You need to practice bringing the leg over the withers first; then you can cross over during any time and at any gait.

Once you have mastered riding sidesaddle, try going around the world.

In this exercise, you start off facing ahead, cross one leg over the horse's withers, keep turning, cross the other leg over the hindquarters, ride backwards, then cross over the hindquarters again, and finally over the withers to be riding straight again.

This exercise is best done on the lounge line, with a friend lounging your horse, and yes, it can be done at all gaits.

These exercises test and push your balance. Be sure to wear your helmet every time. Expect to slide off sometimes. When you do find yourself sliding, try to ball up and roll instead of hitting the ground with legs or arms.

Do not be embarrassed about falling or sliding off! Every horseback rider slides off sometimes. Good riders just get back on.

If your fall is hard, stay still on the ground. Breathe. Wiggle your toes and fingers. If that does not hurt, move your ankles and wrist. If that does not hurt, move your elbows and knees. If that does not hurt, move your shoulders and hips. If that does not hurt, move your neck and head.

If all is pain free, get yourself up, dust yourself off, and try again.

The goal is to learn how to feel your horse, and to notice how slight shifts in your weight create different movements by the horse. Remember how your horse reacts to the different shifts in your weight.

Use the weight distribution of your seat bones and shoulders to communicate with the horse.

Have fun and experiment and play. Explore what you and your horse can do when you move with each other.

Then, one day, Pegasus will come.

So, you want to ride Pegasus. Good for you!
It is nice to have a dream or two.
But this dream is tricky, for soon you will see
That most people in Pegasus do not believe.
Hold fast, hold true, for soon you will know.
Every horse is Pegasus when he can move free.